COSMIC PROVERBS

Pietro di Vietri

iUniverse®

COSMIC PROVERBS

iUniverse books may be ordered through booksellers or by contacting:

iUniverse
1663 Liberty Drive
Bloomington, IN 47403
www.iuniverse.com
844-349-9409

ISBN: 978-1-6632-2797-3 (sc)
ISBN: 978-1-6632-2825-3 (hc)
ISBN: 978-1-6632-2798-0 (e)

Library of Congress Control Number: 2021917681

Print information available on the last page.

iUniverse rev. date: 12/28/2021

TO ELON MUSK
AND ALL THOSE WHO
HAVE A VISION FOR
THE FUTURE.

CONTENTS

INTRODUCTION TO PROVERBS

Proverbs are short, incisive thoughts, or meaningful meditations that express a truth, most of the time of a practical nature or a philosophical tenet.

There is agreat variety of proverbs in content and length, composed by many people, frompoets to emperors, like these by the Roman Emperor Marcus Aurelius (121-180AD) in his famous work Meditations:

What is not good for the swarm is not good for the bee. (Book VI, 54)

You should not be irritated by things, because they do not care. (Book VII, 38) and a more extensive one:

Meditate frequently on the interlocking of all things in the world and on their mutual relationship. For in a way, all things intertwine with each other and in this sense all are friends with each other; for one thing follows the other in order, as the result of the continuous vibration that thrills though all things and the unity of all being. (Book VI, 38) (Meditations, Planeta De Agostini, 1995, Buenos Aires, Argentina).

To take another case, the reflections of Arthur Schopenhauer are both philosophically interesting and quite elaborate. The same can be said of the Proverbs and Songs of Antonio Machado, which are also poetically beautiful. The popular genre constitutes the majority of proverbs in existence worldwide, being

part of the oral tradition. They are anonymous and created
by the people as a humorous, ironic or critical response,
most of the time to specific circumstances. For example:
Dress me slowly because I am in a hurry. (attributed to Napoleon)
These are called short sayings be they Chinese,
Arab, or Mexican, and they abound
in each country as a popular reaction to the behavior of their
rulers. They make up a sparkling segment of popular philosophy.

The majority of proverbs express practical, moral, political,
military or religious truths. The oldest ones are found in all
ancient civilizations, whether Sumerian, Persian, Chinese, Indian,
Babylonian, or Egyptian. More modern examples are the Hebraic,
the Christian, and the Arabic. Each tradition copies, adopts,
reiterates and develops proverbs based on its myths and culture.
Sometimes understanding them requires knowing their context.
In the Chinese civilization they are referred to as phenomena
of nature, government, wars and feelings. For example:
One does not need a lantern when the sun or moon is shining.
No irrigators are needed when the garden
has rain. (The legendary Emperor
Yao offers his Crown to Minister Xu Yu, c. 2300 BC.)
Traditional:
Pioneers plant trees, but the latecomers rest in the shade.
A clear conscience is the greatest shield.
Hurting others will hurt oneself.
Bamboo will bend in the wind. (i.e. it will
change with the times, but not
break)
I hope that you will remove the weeds that
obstruct my mind. (Used to ask
for advice or education)
Your kindness is engraved on my bones.
(As an expression of gratitude)

These are from Confucius (Spring and Autumn Period):
He who speaks without modesty will find it
difficult to make his words good.
Do not treat others as you would not like to be treated.
Do not worry if others do not understand
you. Worry if you do not
understand them.
A tyrannical government is worse than a man-eating tiger.
From Li Bo, Tang Dynasty: Life is just a dream.

The Hebraic proverbs, like the Christian and Muslim traditions, almost always refer to a higher being or principle, respect or fear of which ensures wisdom. This does not mean that these cultures did not have popular proverbs, but that the ones that have influenced the conscience of the West are those included in the so-called *sacred texts.* In certain cases these are commands or advice, with the format: If you do this, then ... Your obedience will be a reward for long life, peace and the good opinion of others. They are considered wise sayings, many attributed to Solomon. They are actually anonymous and come from earlier sources of Middle Eastern wisdom. Attribution of authorship, like heroic acts to kings, was common in the ancient world.
About the Book of Proverbs, The New
Oxford Annotated Bible says:
The book is typical of the literature on Hebrew wisdom and the area of the Middle East, especially Egypt. In fact, a large number of specialists agree that Prov. 22.17–23.11 is dependent on the Instructions of the Egyptian sage Amen-Em-Ope, c. 1100 BCE. At that time there were no copyright laws and appropriation was commonplace. (Today the custom continues, but as an obligatory courtesy the source is cited.) The orientation of the Book of Proverbs was macho-elitist, aimed at educating young men in adult responsibilities: Therefore, its main focus is on a masculine world.

In the biblical case the foundation of the proverbs is in the law, fear and punishment. A moral approach based on religious beliefs is clearly evidenced:

The beginning of wisdom is the fear of the Lord. (Prov. 1:7)

Here we must ask the fear of Jehovah according to whom?

Some, unfortunately, have become obsolete, such as:

Listen, my son, to your father's instruction, and do not despise your mothe's direction (Prov. 1:8). Fewer and fewer children listen to their parents. Today, they listen more to the visual and electronic media than to their parents.

Many proverbs incorporate beauty, wisdom, and age-old knowledge:

Mercy and truth never depart from you;
tie them around your neck, write
them on the tablets of your heart. (Prov. 3:3)

Don't be wise in your own opinion; fear the
Lord, and turn away from evil;
because it will be medicine for your body
and refreshment for your bones.
(Prov. 3:7–8)

As we see, the value of obeying is not just about not engaging in bad behavior; it also promotes good health. Of course, reading this book, like all others, is recommended. This therapeutic concept is reiterated in other proverbs. For example:

My son, pay attention to my words… Because they are life to those who find them and medicine to their whole body. (Prov. 4: 20/22).

The machismo is clear when warning against the strange woman:

For the lips of a strange woman drip honey, and her palate is softer than oil; but her end is bitter as wormwood, sharp as a two-edged sword. Her feet descend to death; her steps lead to Sheol (the afterlife of the wicked). (Prov. 5:3–5)

Apart from the literal meaning, I do not want to omit the symbolic meaning of the strange woman referred to in the religion of the Baals. Moreover, we must not forget that, since Genesis, women have been held responsible for the Fall of man by taking the apple or the forbidden fruit. This discriminatory verdict, which passed to Christianity and Islam, has been a form of silent violence against women for centuries. Without a doubt, biblical proverbs also promote intelligence, wisdom and friendship, except with respect to women. Those who doubt the validity of this assertion may read the seventh chapter on the tricks of the harlots, which contains

such concepts about the foreign woman:

Then a woman comes toward him, decked out like a prostitute, wile of heart. She is loud and wayward (Prov.7: 10–11). Unlike Chinese proverbs, the Book of Proverbs condemns wine and cider. It is correct to say that the last chapter (31) is dedicated to the virtuous woman, but strangely asks:Who will find her?; In other words, she exists, but is almost impossible to find! Then, the praise is non-existent.

During the Roman Empire with the confluence of cultures there were many proverbs. Any reader will find in the writings of Seneca (4 BC-65AD), especially The Golden Book, as in The Seven Books of Wisdom, many beautiful proverbs. I have already mentioned Marcus Aurelius, who, like many enlightened Chinese emperors, expressed his wise thoughts or meditations brilliantly. In the philosophical writings of the philosopher Epictetus (50- 135 AD), a former slave, memorable proverbs are found. Here are two:
Correct your passions before they punish you.
And this one, which is as apposite as almost two millennia ago:

No one who is a lover of money, a lover of pleasure,
a lover of glory, can be a lover of humanity;
only he who is a lover of virtue can be.

It is interesting how these concepts passed to the heirs of the empire, especially the Anglo-Saxons. Jewish folk proverbs are funnier, wittier and more sparkling because, as a minority group, they lived in the midst of many cultures from which they both took and contributed something. The Hebrews, under Communist ideology, developed expressions that are incomprehensible to those who did not experience that state of oppression. But it was humor and synthetic wisdom that made life tolerable for them. The popular Arab proverbs have a rather subtle grace, as they had to be careful not to offend aspects of their dogmatic religion. My English relatives used to speak with proverbs constantly, demonstrating how powerful they are as a reference in daily life. Foremost was:
You can lead a horse to water, but you can't make him drink.
They said it about people who are given advice, an instruction or a book, but cannot be forced to learn. I cite others:
A chain is as strong as the weakest link.
Actions speak louder than words.
God helps those who help themselves.
When in Rome you do like the Romans.
Treat others as you would like them to treat you.
(Here we see an echo of Confucius.)

India is also a fountain of proverbs. I remember:
What is now in the past was once in the future.
and two from Mahatma Gandhi:
Every dog is a tiger in his own street.
A guilty conscience is a hidden enemy.

As we can see, many proverbs are common to all mankind and their origins can be traced to China, India, Babylon or Persia. This is because their brevity makes them easy to remember, and, like jokes, they adapt easily to different languages and continents.

There was an old saying that gave impulse to
the proverbs to go from mind to mind:
Take me by your side, I will be your guide.

Among those coming from popular poetry, I think that those coming from the countryside are simple and joyful:
He is happy as a dog with two tails.

I must apologize for not including proverbs from Russia, South Africa, Mexico, but the purpose of the introduction has been only to show the universal use of this cultural and literary form. It is my wish that these concepts serve as sources of inspiration and for meditation, as well as entertainment.

PRINCIPLES AND PURPOSES

Purpose

The cosmos exists because it's alive.

★ ★ ★ ★

In the cosmos, there will always be more or less favorable conditions of life.

★ ★ ★ ★

Each individual form of life finds its cosmic way to adapt.

Not everything is part of or should be included in algorithms.

★ ★ ★ ★

Stars are only sparks in eternity.

★ ★ ★ ★

Galactic ships can speed up by stellar wind.

Cosmic rays can help or wreck what they find along the way.

★ ★ ★ ★

Going outside the solar system, we earn a new vision of the universe, but we lose the helioplasm's protective shield.

★ ★ ★ ★

In the cosmos, we don't see what protects us,
and we don't hear rays that damage us.

The same spirit that sustains and invigorates
life on earth will do so in the cosmos.

★ ★ ★ ★

For long flights, cyborgs are going to replace humans.

★ ★ ★ ★

Body, brain, and machine will be one.

In space, it's not "to be or not to be" but
"to be what or to be not."

★ ★ ★ ★

Moving with purpose avoids going adrift.

★ ★ ★ ★

Great expectations don't skip small steps; they need them.

The space argonaut will seek neither the Golden Fleece nor the Holy Grail; he will seek his cosmic destiny.

★ ★ ★ ★

Some individuals know where they are going; others just run behind.

★ ★ ★ ★

Everything good is worth the effort.

A sensible law must foresee the social, economic, environmental, and cosmic consequences.

★ ★ ★ ★

You are not rewarded for what you think you know but for what you can prove.

★ ★ ★ ★

Responsibility can be stressful or invigorating; it is a personal choice.

The cosmic individual will be able to move in different planetary times, but his mind will have to be kept in precise cosmic times.

★ ★ ★ ★

Opportunities do not depend on luck;
they are created by hard work.

★ ★ ★ ★

What is not used is lost, and if it is abused it is also lost.

Places and activities do not define our destiny or our being.

★ ★ ★ ★

With our vision fixed on the goal we
enjoy every step of the journey.

★ ★ ★ ★

Anger can lead to defeat faster than a superior enemy.

When your principles are aligned, all areas of your life are ordered.

★ ★ ★ ★

Favorable circumstances always exist, but we
have to produce opportunities ourselves.

★ ★ ★ ★

Even the worst failure can turn into a great success.

Goals are achieved with will and concentration of energy.

★ ★ ★ ★

If you like to collect things, you must be willing to deal with dust.

★ ★ ★ ★

An inveterate optimist sees continual
opportunity behind constant trouble.

Too much attachment to good results can prevent them.

★ ★ ★ ★

Circumstances don't just happen; people contribute to them with thoughts, feelings, or actions.

★ ★ ★ ★

If you need a law, then you will need a judge.

A human law is the imposition of the will of the few over many.

★ ★ ★ ★

Honest legislators make laws to solve people's problems.
Cunning legislators make laws to employ lawyers.

★ ★ ★ ★

It is easier to hit the mark when the prize does not distract us.

Wealth achieved through generations' work
is appropriated by a lawyer in court.

★ ★ ★ ★

History is the synthesis of human ambitions and aspirations.

★ ★ ★ ★

When ambitions for profit or power destroy the earth,
those who inhabit it suffer, and those who profit condemn
themselves by killing the future of their children.

Never give toy guns to a child; it can be the seed with which one day he can kill someone.

★ ★ ★ ★

Short-term power depends on strength; in the medium term, it depends on intelligence; in the long run on wisdom; but for infinity, it depends on spirituality.

★ ★ ★ ★

During youth, there are always individuals willing to die for the truth, since it is harder to live for it than to die for it.

Those who truly love are not intimidated
by threats, dangers, or sacrifices.

★ ★ ★ ★

People who fail are those who possess ambition for
success, rather than a passion for a noble life.

★ ★ ★ ★

While history never repeats itself, its events never
cease to resonate in human memory.

To be successful, trust your intuition and feelings first and then your knowledge.

★ ★ ★ ★

It is very human to prefer convenience to truth.

★ ★ ★ ★

If you want to live with dignity, you must take risks.

When wishes blind us, they make us lose our reason
and so our way.

★ ★ ★ ★

We have to be 100 percent honest with ourselves
if we want to be honest with others.

★ ★ ★ ★

We must learn to plan from the future to act in the present.

Abandoning initiatives leads to many failures.

★ ★ ★ ★

Religious politics is the claim of uniting the greatest number of people under a principle that the owners of power call god.

★ ★ ★ ★

The true hero is not the one who defeats others but the one who triumphs over his own passions and false beliefs.

In a circular world, we dissolve horizons,
constantly creating new ones.

★ ★ ★ ★

Revolutions promise what the people want
to hear and can never deliver.

★ ★ ★ ★

We improve the world when we first change ourselves,
and then we become engines of change.

We must beware of the revolutions that defeat tyrants and empower criminals.

★ ★ ★ ★

The consequences of our actions should be our guide.

★ ★ ★ ★

The world is full of violence because we do not make the effort to fill it with empathy, justice, and love.

The creative principle renews us in perfection, beauty, and health.

★ ★ ★ ★

Controlling emotions is like controlling a volcano or a tsunami—impossible. With foresight, though, their consequences can be avoided.

★ ★ ★ ★

Each step is always a step toward our destiny.

Patiently educating shy children transforms their mental circuits and strengthens them, enabling them to fly at high altitudes.

★ ★ ★ ★

Before lifting your foot, think about where you will put it. Each step reconfigures your brain, your path, and the final destination.

★ ★ ★ ★

Those who demand a purer world must begin with their own heart.

If proclaiming intentions to the wind, other minds can interfere in the expected results.

★ ★ ★ ★

Each individual, at some point, is the best in society and does not require everyone to know it.

★ ★ ★ ★

Justice brings health to society, just as food nourishes the body.

Those who wish to hide must learn from their cats.

★ ★ ★ ★

Charity must liberate without creating dependency or bondage.

★ ★ ★ ★

Noble ideals do not impose a goal; they only light the way.

Wretched the artist in need of the government to be famous.

★ ★ ★ ★

People who complain about the century in which they live did not have the misfortune to live in a previous one.

★ ★ ★ ★

Truth suffers less when lies are clear.

Obstacles alert you to continue on the same path.

★ ★ ★ ★

Complying with the law in whose approval
we participated makes us free.

★ ★ ★ ★

Insults are dangerous boomerangs—they come
back in a rage at those who throw them.

For violent fanatics, the worst punishment is the peace of paradise.

★ ★ ★ ★

Power perverts when it transforms sheep into wolves.

★ ★ ★ ★

Without principles, good or evil can be justified as the wind blows.

When the passions rule, mind can be the worst enemy.

★ ★ ★ ★

If you want to be served well, get the attention of the waiter's eye.

★ ★ ★ ★

People cling to their views until the evidence shakes them.

Everything that is gained through violence is lost through violence.

★ ★ ★ ★

If you fall, get up thinking about how to move and where to go.

★ ★ ★ ★

Group patriotism is treason to all humanity.

Excessive expectations produce setbacks and failures.

★ ★ ★ ★

The principle of freedom is neutral: It does not stop you from going to hell; nor does it push you to go to heaven.

★ ★ ★ ★

When the media did not exist, criminals hid their crimes; now they commit them to become famous.

Lusts and desires are tied to vices, harmful foods, toxic people, or unnecessary objects.

★ ★ ★ ★

The fanatic is a saint who believes himself to possess a divine and unique truth, which is why he is blind and deaf to any other possibility.

★ ★ ★ ★

A person with self-contradictory ideas works to his ruin.

Giving wealth to people without merit makes them morally poor.

★ ★ ★ ★

Individuals obsessed with failure are ultimately successful failures.

★ ★ ★ ★

Peace does not come from fighting hatred but from
cultivating empathy, kindness, and harmony.

The only legitimate origin of law is duty. Duty validates the dignity of just laws.

★ ★ ★ ★

Freedom of conscience does not justify damaging the conscience of others.

★ ★ ★ ★

Where the lazy complain about limitations, entrepreneurs see opportunities.

Life is given to us to dignify it.

★ ★ ★ ★

Those who first deny the history of the
peoples then deny their rights.

★ ★ ★ ★

Technology overcomes old limitations by creating new disparities.

★ ★ ★ ★

It is not our appearance but our choices that make us different.

SCIENCE AND TECHNOLOGY

The void is always full.

★ ★ ★ ★

Being will be at one in body, brain, and machine.

★ ★ ★ ★

The best-known equation in science ($E = mc^2$) was not the result of an investigation but of a dream and imagination.

We will know the universe following the simplicity and beauty of science.

★ ★ ★ ★

To create a new theory, it is necessary to dethrone and go beyond the old ones.

★ ★ ★ ★

Each discovery demands a critical amount of patience.

The universe exists because it is alive; therefore, life can develop and adapt to the most extreme conditions.

★ ★ ★ ★

In the universe, each form of life finds its way to adapt.

★ ★ ★ ★

If all the emotions were included in an algorithm it could explode!

The helioplasm envelops us like a silkworm cocoon. Leaving it does not turn us into star butterflies; cosmic rays can burn our wings.

★ ★ ★ ★

Stellar wind and cosmic rays can speed up or wreck galactic ships.

★ ★ ★ ★

Going for a walk outside the solar system gives us a new vision of the universe but removes the protective shield of helioplasm.

We do not see what protects us; nor do we
hear the aggression of cosmic rays.

★ ★ ★ ★

Time is not long or short; it depends on how we live it.

★ ★ ★ ★

The efficient arch works on tension and flexibility.

Time is born of movement; it is the slave of movement, and without movement, it dies.

★ ★ ★ ★

The acceleration of velocity contracts mass and time and, thus, extends the life of travelers through space.

★ ★ ★ ★

Time can speed up, slowed down, stopped, or eliminated but never turned back, even if the mind does so.

Science is the tool by which to find constants in the flow of events.

★ ★ ★ ★

Not all changes occur at the same speed.

★ ★ ★ ★

If scientists cannot predict when events will occur, they should at least accurately record them when they happen.

The art in science consists of knowing how to hide irrational sides.

★ ★ ★ ★

When people get sick, they look for exterior causes to blame. —whether it's that someone infected them, wind or rain sun or sand: in fact, they blame everyone and everything except themselves for lowering the moral and spiritual shield of their immune protection.

★ ★ ★ ★

In cosmos or chaos, nothing is still.

Theoretical climate forecasting models show that reality
is more complex than the models can contemplate.

★ ★ ★ ★

Clouds and wind are chronic rebels and
sometimes show their bad temper.

★ ★ ★ ★

An individual experience does not determine a universal law.

The researcher who satisfies her curiosity with new discoveries is happy as a babe.

★ ★ ★ ★

There was a creation myth for every civilization. Now science buries them in silence.

★ ★ ★ ★

The uncertainty principle maintains that it's impossible to know precisely the speed and position of a subatomic particle at the same time. The same uncertainty applies to politics and lovers.

Knowledge is one, but we approach it in small plots.

★ ★ ★ ★

In the empty, dark space of the cosmos lie
answers we've been seeking for millennia.

★ ★ ★ ★

A scientist is the one who, through the use of
abstractions, is able to predict concrete reality.

Either imagination sets us free, or reality will make us its slaves.

★ ★ ★ ★

After the first second of the big bang, the universe had formed; before, it was just an eventuality.

★ ★ ★ ★

Matter and antimatter destroy each other; if they had been the same, the universe would have already disappeared.

An infinitesimal difference of matter over antimatter
causes the entire universe to exist in all its beauty.
Does this explain how an infinitesimal
detail can make us disappear?

★ ★ ★ ★

Science maintains that the origin of matter and the present universe is due to the Higgs boson; without it, we would only be light. What would we do with our shadow?

★ ★ ★ ★

Human capacities have no limits to improve, innovate, or imagine.

Technology can free us or enslave us.

★ ★ ★ ★

Genes provide a basic program; then experience and context stimulate growth and destiny.

★ ★ ★ ★

Mathematics can make fun of us more accurately than people think.

When emotions and thoughts are transformed into biology, they are a vital crossroads for health or disease, discord or harmony.

★ ★ ★ ★

Before the assurances of science, a quota of doubt must be kept.

★ ★ ★ ★

The ultimate purpose of psychology is not to study the psyche but to search for the self behind the forest of thoughts.

In the long run, harmonious science will do the difference.

★ ★ ★ ★

Paradoxical mathematics can produce accurate results.

★ ★ ★ ★

The distance between the parts of the reptilian brain, the emotional and the rational, is millions of years.

Scientific formulas, like good jokes, should be eloquent and short.

★ ★ ★ ★

Discoveries in space will be
perfected on earth.

★ ★ ★ ★

Creativity and imagination prevail over force.

Humans created time; they deified it. Later, Cronos enslaved them.

★ ★ ★ ★

In the world of atoms, there is no
transcendence, only transformation.

★ ★ ★ ★

The "scientific" truths about black holes will
make future generations laugh.

Even the best scientist navigates through trial and error every day.

★ ★ ★ ★

Theories are always perfect; it's reality that rebels against them.

★ ★ ★ ★

There is no need to rush to the future; it will
come peacefully, even if we ignore it.

Reality will reveal itself by fighting against it or by yielding to it.

★ ★ ★ ★

The strength or fragility of a system depends
on the energy that sustains it.

★ ★ ★ ★

The ignorant prefer myths to science.

What we perceive through telescopes is never the thing itself.

★ ★ ★ ★

Only those who do not struggle to overcome obstacles fail.

★ ★ ★ ★

Failures guide investigations where opportunities germinate.

When your shadow matches your figure, by measuring your shadow, you will know your height.

★ ★ ★ ★

Algorithms always existed, but they always needed a mind to make them visible.

★ ★ ★ ★

All systems are susceptible to contagion and immune development.

Rude mistakes can lead to accurate discoveries.

★ ★ ★ ★

Artificial intelligence surpasses human intelligence in calculation speed and in games of chess and poker. Does anyone doubt that it will surpasses humans in other areas? But never in the reasons of the heart, which not even the heart knows.

★ ★ ★ ★

Multiple theories can be developed on the same facts. Things and the world have in themselves a natural meaning, but humans give meaning according to their convenience.

What we see through microscopes is not
what we touch with our hands.

★ ★ ★ ★

DNA is not a language. It is a quantum of
information that is incorporated into each cell.

★ ★ ★ ★

The human body is a concentration of coded information.

In the near future, there will be no need to hack computers;
they will directly hack the individual mind.

★ ★ ★ ★

Hacking will be more than a moral danger;
it will be a criminal action.

★ ★ ★ ★

The human mind cries out for healing.

Public and private cameras around the world will read our behavior and know us better than ourselves.

★ ★ ★ ★

Artificial Intelligence will alter human intelligence and reduce millions to irrelevance.

★ ★ ★ ★

Artificial intelligence may make you believe that someone is "brainstorming" when, in reality, they are changing the brain's circuits.

Defense against cyberattacks will demand inviolable mental shields and sound spiritual principles.

★ ★ ★ ★

Clouds, dreams, visions, intuitions, and imaginations, like the theory of relativity, are real because they produce concrete effects on the world.

★ ★ ★ ★

Technology, from the wheel to the microchip, overcomes old limitations to create new opportunities.

Computers process data; humans give it meaning.

★ ★ ★ ★

Biology is neither future nor destiny; it is history.

★ ★ ★ ★

In a vacuum, what works perfectly are theories–
and sometimes not even that!

★ ★ ★ ★

Since the whole contains the part, don't be surprised
if the part contains the whole, as a free sample.

WELL-BEING AND HAPPINESS

Laughing rejuvenates the blood.

★ ★ ★ ★

Smiling brings joy around you!

★ ★ ★ ★

Well-being is not about maintaining a good balance of the body's atoms, which are always in crazy balance, but about using them creatively to transcend them.

Laugh—the truth often switches sides!

★ ★ ★ ★

Be wary of food where the bathrooms are dirty.

★ ★ ★ ★

Being in very good health means having
reserves for the unexpected.

The here and now is the gift that life offers us.

★ ★ ★ ★

A slave can be a king and a king a slave;
it is a matter of imagination.

★ ★ ★ ★

You will recognize a drunk person; his face is
the color of a perplexed autumn leaf.

With deep motivations, you can get deep results; with superficial motivations, we confuse even the mind itself.

★ ★ ★ ★

Satisfying the desire to possess unnecessary things becomes a heavy burden.

★ ★ ★ ★

Enjoying the present is the way to be amazed all your life.

Happiness is not at odds with wealth.

★ ★ ★ ★

Question the success that does not bring you happiness.

★ ★ ★ ★

Success can be measured by the amount of money
or by the amount of joy, peace, and happiness.

We should be smart about how to heal ourselves
but even wiser in avoiding getting sick.

★ ★ ★ ★

The best doctor and the best patient for your body
is yourself. Be responsible and well qualified!

★ ★ ★ ★

Listen to your body. It speaks to you day and night,
awake and in dreams.

Your body is your Garden of Eden and your battlefield. Do not get drunk from its perfume or perish from the injuries you inflict on yourself.

★ ★ ★ ★

Using contraceptives to separate pleasure from reproduction does not mean killing the germs of virtue and responsibility.

★ ★ ★ ★

Successful is the person for whom failure is an incentive to improve, progress, and take the next step.

Either we face the problems today, or they will run us down tomorrow.

★ ★ ★ ★

The individual is the product of the circumstances he entered and in which he decided to remain.

★ ★ ★ ★

Reality is based on the vision we develop. The progress of humanity depends on how this vision is incorporated into human affairs.

Positive attitudes transform our physiology
and the results of our actions.

★ ★ ★ ★

Wonderful things happen all the time; we must learn to see them.

★ ★ ★ ★

A healthy and altruistic life does not need remedies.

Happiness is not just around the corner; we build it around our way of thinking.

★ ★ ★ ★

Why is it that we don't really know how happy we'll be if we get everything we want? It's not because we don't know what the future will be like but because we don't know what we really want now.

★ ★ ★ ★

Whoever is not an inventor is a slave to inventions.

What we enjoy in the present moment is the postlude of the remembered time and the prelude of the expected time.

★ ★ ★ ★

Let us be happy now, even if suffering, because we do not know if we will have another world.

★ ★ ★ ★

While you overcome suffering, do not postpone happiness.

Happiness is not the gold we possess but the joy we bring.

★ ★ ★ ★

The worst slavery comes from the chains of our traditions.

★ ★ ★ ★

Some people yearn, more than for
happiness, to flee from suffering.

Every time you start something, you will
also leave something behind.

★ ★ ★ ★

If you want to be happy in this world, avoid being trapped.

★ ★ ★ ★

For every published act of evil, there are
millions of ignored acts of kindness.

Everything is simpler than the simplest thing you can imagine.

★ ★ ★ ★

If your life is a meaningless ruin, look at
the thoughts that have ruled you.

★ ★ ★ ★

Considering the food we eat, avoid looking
for remedies for the stomach.

Happiness depends as much on knowing how to enjoy what we have as on what we do without.

★ ★ ★ ★

When anger dominates, reason and harmony disappear.

★ ★ ★ ★

The purpose of avoiding pain, preserving life, and serving others brings delight.

If when you go to play a sport, it's not done with joy, then you're not playing a sport.

★ ★ ★ ★

The myth of the hero represents the triumphant human capacity to free ourselves from our fears.

★ ★ ★ ★

The holidays begin when the connection with routine is really cut off.

We progress when we flow with the future.

★ ★ ★ ★

Human beauty is paradoxical: It mixes uniqueness with diversity to generate a renewed beauty.

★ ★ ★ ★

Eating calmly is polite and helps digestion.

Better poor and worthy than rich and shameless.

★ ★ ★ ★

Spontaneous happiness is a grace from heaven.

★ ★ ★ ★

Mystical experiences generate ecstasy even in pain.

The best reality is the one that allows us to live happily.

★ ★ ★ ★

Happiness is a dream; that's why sleep pleases us all our lives.

★ ★ ★ ★

The years cannot be extended, but the quality of life can.

Happiness seems impossible; that's why we constantly look for it.

★ ★ ★ ★

Expanding your quality of life extends your years.

★ ★ ★ ★

Running fast as a young man makes you happy; running as an adult brings joy; finally, in old age each step generates bliss because the triumph is not in running but in reaching the goal.

Without bitterness, would you appreciate the sweetness of life?

★ ★ ★ ★

Happy is the person adapting to changing circumstance creatively.

★ ★ ★ ★

Joy in solitude expands the soul; shared joy expands friendship.

Those who are not happy with their season can turn the hourglass and drop water or sand, but they will not be able to put their feet in their heads.

★ ★ ★ ★

For Aristotle, living well was living in society, in that noble good happiness consisted. From there, it comes to us that happiness is full when it is shared.

★ ★ ★ ★

Doing your own will closes the door to happiness.

Addiction to sugar and salt can be as dangerous
as driving with your eyes closed.

★ ★ ★ ★

The flapping of the smallest bird leaves its design in the sky. We ignore them like millions of things we don't see.

★ ★ ★ ★

Sow happiness in your garden; its cultivation
will give joy even to the stars.

ROBOTICS

Sapiens create robots from their own bodies.

★ ★ ★ ★

Biological robots are limited by their own biology.

★ ★ ★ ★

The belief that sapiens are free, considering their limitations is the major lie on earth.

The human algorithm consumes a lot of energy to function indefinitely.

★ ★ ★ ★

A robot works without breathing or suffering.

★ ★ ★ ★

Without limit of body and brain, the human would be conscious life as it was before birth.

Biological robots consume so much energy
that they are devouring the earth.

★ ★ ★ ★

In space, robots will be the best assistants for humans.

★ ★ ★ ★

The difference between a robot and a human is that the human
is an unsatisfied animal.

The cosmos awaits us; we leave our ideas and carry our oxygen and joy.

★ ★ ★ ★

Robots work with memory and intelligence,
humans with the heart and dreams.

★ ★ ★ ★

The brain is a limited robot.
Mind instead is unlimited and not localized.

Robots work on the basis of cybernetics;
without feedback, they perish.

★ ★ ★ ★

The stars have planets and satellites of different apparent sexes, as humans have sons, daughters, and granddaughters, no surprises.

★ ★ ★ ★

A robot will always do, even if it never knows why it does.

The first law of robotics says that a robot should never harm a human. That does not prevent the human from harming himself.

★ ★ ★ ★

In the cosmos, telepathy is not an ability to despise.

★ ★ ★ ★

A robot will never understand that it has no real existence.

★ ★ ★ ★

With all its imitations, a robot will go where the human cannot.

NATURE

Cats are mysterious because—being curious—
they never confess their philosophy.

★ ★ ★ ★

In autumn, trees love the wind; he is the
best hairdresser they know.

★ ★ ★ ★

Trees converse through their roots, send their messages
through the wind, and record the hours with their shadow.

The rose was born from a dream from which no one can wake it up.

★ ★ ★ ★

Nature can be altered but not improved. She knows how to transform and improve herself.

★ ★ ★ ★

Rains and floods remind us that, in life, there are more "depressions" than we think.

Nature does not waste time on vanities, because even the vain are part of a final purpose.

★ ★ ★ ★

Nature heals because it's authentic.

★ ★ ★ ★

Admire roses without playing with them—unless you want to feel their thorns.

When the climate changes, we must change
the clouds in our mental paradigms.

★ ★ ★ ★

If you look at a cloud, think that it could be water, gas, or ice.
Don't be fooled; it is a mask from the carnival of nature.

★ ★ ★ ★

We are always amazed by unknown landscapes.

Natural reality has no ideals or doctrines, only many ideologues.

★ ★ ★ ★

The soil embraces the seed to protect it and provide it with the means to unfold its destiny.

★ ★ ★ ★

Overprotected children beget fearful adults.

Not being sweet is healthy.

★ ★ ★ ★

Clay does not produce amphorae or art by itself; it needs a generative mind and working hands.

★ ★ ★ ★

Delicious foods can have harmful effects.

What is convenient for humans can be a disaster for nature.

★ ★ ★ ★

Time is a tireless grave digger; it buries day after day.

★ ★ ★ ★

Animals do not use timers and are more accurate than humans. Was something lost in evolution?

Those who never planted a seed are dangerously ignorant.

★ ★ ★ ★

Nature is wise without theories or arguments.

★ ★ ★ ★

The biosphere thrives by overcoming
imbalances and seeking harmonies.

The environment does not have a plan, because she has an infinite capacity for improvisation.

★ ★ ★ ★

Because of her infinite capacity for improvisation, nature does not need a plan. She loves trees for their greenery, their fruits, their dark shade dancing with the wind.

★ ★ ★ ★

The process of nature is magical: It reveals itself from a photon to a black hole and from an amoeba to a human being. It builds, de-builds, and disappears.

Humans create dogmas, and nature responds, denying them.

★ ★ ★ ★

Nature is a mixture of harmony and dissonance,
and from it comes modern music.

★ ★ ★ ★

History like nature is without arguments, principles, or ends—it is!

If you've seen the smile of a rose, you've
seen the splendor of the world.

★ ★ ★ ★

Riches extracted from the earth today may
turn into catastrophic losses tomorrow.

★ ★ ★ ★

The shaman questioning nature receives a shamanic
answer; a doctor gets a medical response. Both are
to cure. Nature is generous to everyone!

★ ★ ★ ★

Knowing how to look at landscapes enriches and inspires.

COSMIC

From space, the world is a jewel without borders.

★ ★ ★ ★

Whoever can speak to the sea can also speak to the cosmos.

★ ★ ★ ★

Chaos poses the questions, in the cosmos the answers.

For complete temporal freedom, consciousness must dwell in spiritual metaphysics.

★ ★ ★ ★

The cosmic being carries in its cells the evolution of the entire universe.

★ ★ ★ ★

We are what is to come; the rest is already past.

When the mind touches the object, reality is transformed.

★ ★ ★ ★

Reality is recreated when it is not observed.

★ ★ ★ ★

When humans measure their life in cosmic time, they will understand the universal dimension of their existence.

Archimedes is a good example that if after thinking in depth no answer comes, the best thing is to stop thinking, take a good bath, and let nature bring the solution!

★ ★ ★ ★

If the atoms were still, the universe would be at peace but dead.

★ ★ ★ ★

For planets, movement is essential. For humans it's important. But for consciousness, what counts is stillness.

You will be able to see only what you have already understood.

★ ★ ★ ★

Most scholars believe—in their ignorance—that the world is defined only by their sphere of knowledge.

★ ★ ★ ★

A black hole can have lucid laws.

The existence of meta-universes cannot be proved if the possibility of their existence is not accepted first. In fact, to prove the existence of something, the hypothesis that "that something exists" is necessary. Nobody can prove the "nonexistence" of "nonexistence."

★ ★ ★ ★

Small causes can produce gigantic effects.

★ ★ ★ ★

The humans like to go to the darkest places of the universe; they have an irresistible appeal.

While you rest, dreams play in your mind
as visitors from other worlds.

★ ★ ★ ★

Cosmic phenomena are beautiful in their wild unpredictability.

★ ★ ★ ★

The ancient mariners looked to the sky and established their course by the order of the stars. Today, the course is fixed by listening to sky's satellite signals. In one way or another, navigators are governed by the sky.

The sky is a mirror that doesn't give back your image but, rather, transports it to the space without horizon.

★ ★ ★ ★

Know that all of reality will be possible when the barriers of time have been obliterated.

★ ★ ★ ★

What we see is tainted by what we think we know.

When our mind faces the unknown, it associates it with the known as a way to avoid losing control of its reality.

★ ★ ★ ★

In space, no one falls, but it's easy to get lost.

★ ★ ★ ★

The only constant in the universe is not light but movement.

We are in "the now," without ever losing sight of the future.

★ ★ ★ ★

Don't overestimate the good or bad impact of future events, like going to the moon or other galaxies. In the end, they will be part of normalcy.

★ ★ ★ ★

The present is what we apprehend from the future; then we cast it into oblivion.

In the human imagination, there are mysteries vaster than the cosmos; that suggests that, behind the cosmos, there is something else.

★ ★ ★ ★

The universe is a theorem of whose proof we are its greatest unknown.

★ ★ ★ ★

Small imperfections would not matter if they did not spread throughout the cosmos.

We see what we want to see because, in the process of looking, we erase everything else.

★ ★ ★ ★

If we change our obsessive way of looking, a new universe will appear in focus.

★ ★ ★ ★

All humans possess abilities, but few have the courage to enter the unknown.

We are the result of a universe expanding into the future, the result of an event on the past horizon.

★ ★ ★ ★

We don't know the origin of the matter that produced the big bang. What's worse is that we don't know who provided the space to allow such an event.

★ ★ ★ ★

Space and the universe contain each other.

Faced with artificial intelligence and robots,
humans can degrade or ascend.

★ ★ ★ ★

Fish do not exist without the seas. The seas do not exist without planets. Planets do not exist without stars. Stars do not exist without galaxies and galaxies do not exist without the cosmos. When you talk about fish, don't forget that you are talking about the cosmos.

★ ★ ★ ★

Life expands with the projects we undertake.

Stars, like orgasms, don't last forever.

★ ★ ★ ★

The representation of the world is not the world; it is what the mind believes of it.

★ ★ ★ ★

Time is a ghost whose power over us depends on the reality we give to it.

If you travel enough, you can find your
ultimate homeland—your conscience.

★ ★ ★ ★

Each day can reveal our destiny to us if we open our eyes to bliss.

★ ★ ★ ★

Heaven is a vast mystery open to all.

The unity of consciousness and the universe is irreducible.

★ ★ ★ ★

An explorer is not surprised by the unknown;
he's ready to adapt and change his being.

★ ★ ★ ★

No distance is long, no distance is short;
both are in the same circle of being.

The universe is another river that flows with us in it.

★ ★ ★ ★

Generating a dynamic vision of tomorrow, we renew our life today.

★ ★ ★ ★

What we do not see is vastly superior to what we perceive.

The universe we see today is not the one we will see tomorrow. Do not miss the opportunity to contemplate it, or you will not know where you existed.

★ ★ ★ ★

The idea of multiverses accommodates the existence of beings with parallel lives ignoring each other without taking offense.

★ ★ ★ ★

The universe expands at a higher speed than light because the universe loves to give it space.

The future destiny depends less on fate and will than on the law of gravity.

★ ★ ★ ★

For those whose life is a perpetual flight, it is heroic to stop to contemplate it.

★ ★ ★ ★

The universe is unlimited because unlimited are the thoughts that it must harbor.

The rivers cannot be stopped without consequences because the sun likes to swim in its currents.

★ ★ ★ ★

The fact of not perceiving does not mean not existing; this is a cosmic principle.

★ ★ ★ ★

Everything that exists is hermetically related.

A life is not enough to think deeply about
the chaos and the cosmos.

★ ★ ★ ★

Discovering the intangible allows us to better
discern the vast visible universe.

★ ★ ★ ★

We are more than what the senses allow us to think;
we are what consciousness allows us to be.

Invisible universes move in front of and around our senses.

★ ★ ★ ★

Beyond the incorporeal and subtle worlds,
everything is imagination and conjecture.

★ ★ ★ ★

The most beautiful part of the cosmos is in you.

In the flourishing garden of the universe,
silence perfumes the soul with peace.

★ ★ ★ ★

What we see from space, we ignore on earth, and what
we see from earth may be irrelevant in space.

★ ★ ★ ★

From space, everything is more beautiful
and, at the same time, more distant.

Any mystery is part of a bigger mystery.

★ ★ ★ ★

Circling the earth from space, there is no time to smell the perfume of flowers or hear the sound of the waves of the sea.

★ ★ ★ ★

For the cosmos, gravity is theology.

What we perceive of the universe happened millions of years ago. Our knowledge is delayed according to the distance from the facts.

★ ★ ★ ★

What we see is tainted by what we think we know.

★ ★ ★ ★

The universe mirrors the evolution of our understanding.

The cognitive system captures the entire universe but discerns only what its limited evolution allows.

★ ★ ★ ★

The cosmos is friendly as long as we are friends of its order.

★ ★ ★ ★

If we look at the cosmos with our little eyes, and they are part of the cosmos, aren't we looking into each other's eyes?

We are in the universe as dreamers dreaming
of a reality outside of ourselves.

★ ★ ★ ★

In space, we are as free as gravity allows us to be.

★ ★ ★ ★

A planet cannot be understood through the beliefs of another.

Close encounters in the cosmos are millions of light-years away.

★ ★ ★ ★

In space, there are more phenomena than
mind and computers can process.

★ ★ ★ ★

Metaphysically, life began in chaos, but
it will flourish in the cosmos.

What we see now—in space—we will not see in the future.

★ ★ ★ ★

The distance depends on possibilities.

★ ★ ★ ★

The body of the universe undergoes explosions
to keep the immune system alive.

Overcoming the law of gravity is part of
human freedom and destiny.

★ ★ ★ ★

A fact can be wave and particle in two different places at the same time. It is the way of reality to show where you were and where you will be without getting bored.

★ ★ ★ ★

Paradoxes greater than the cosmos exist in the imagination of men.

In the human imagination, there are more vast mysteries than the cosmos. That suggests that behind the cosmos there is another mind.

★ ★ ★ ★

If the earth becomes a circular prison, humanity will seek its freedom on other worlds.

★ ★ ★ ★

Everything that exists flows with change.

In space, there are no fences or borders.

★ ★ ★ ★

Whoever treats the universe with love will thus be treated. Whoever treats the universe with displeasure, the same will he be treated. This is the quintessential cosmic rule.

★ ★ ★ ★

Yes, the universe contains the cosmos and chaos.

No world is strange if you can be there.

★ ★ ★ ★

The future of humanity will depend less on its physical structure than it does on its spiritual essence.

★ ★ ★ ★

We are pilgrims of history and space.

The cosmic human will leave the dust of the earth
and incorporate in their DNA the dust of the stars.

★ ★ ★ ★

Nebulae are made up of gases, stardust,
plasma, and our ignorance.

★ ★ ★ ★

Humans will not think about becoming extinct until they
have faced trials and errors and become cosmic species.
When there is a reason, there is a will to leave
our own home to go to another world.

The galactic age is forming cosmic consciousness as the only reality.

★ ★ ★ ★

Odysseus, Columbus, and Vasco da Gama went on adventures with the goal of returning to their origin. Planetary explorers assume the possibility of changing their mental genesis never to return.

★ ★ ★ ★

Not all children today let their eyes be devoured by electronic screens; some dream of touching the stars.

Humanity—insignificant in the universe—will go out to become a planetary destination among the stars.

★ ★ ★ ★

The innate desire to break boundaries drives the individual forward and upward.

★ ★ ★ ★

We go because we want to go; it is also possible that our stellar ancestors are whispering to us, "We are waiting for you."

As humanity overcomes the law of gravity,
it will also overcome the space-time dimension.

★ ★ ★ ★

A galactic political system must apply cybernetics and
living individuals' feedback to serve efficiently.

★ ★ ★ ★

The space debris is not going anywhere; it remains there
to greet us as a reminder that we are a dirty species.

On the hidden face of cosmologies, there was always hope and determination to continue the cosmic adventure.

★ ★ ★ ★

Lying on earth, humans cannot avoid the wonder of the heavens dreaming to reach the stars.

★ ★ ★ ★

Lack of gravity makes sex laxer and love stronger.

Spying on the future from earth took us to space. Spying on the future from space will take us to other dimensions.

★ ★ ★ ★

There is more life in space than on earth.

★ ★ ★ ★

The cosmos contains hidden gems, treasures no human can even imagine.

The universe is an intelligent entity that has created conscious beings—cocreators of the world.

★ ★ ★ ★

Robots can be smarter than humans even if they are not self-aware.

★ ★ ★ ★

When the music of the universe resounds in the heart, our being acquires the vision of cosmic unity.

Many planets cross each other's orbit and never greet, they belong to different times.

★ ★ ★ ★

The mind is a neutral processor; it operates like any computer, with all kinds of information independent of the source and consequences.

★ ★ ★ ★

If we get lost among robots, one day we will be one of them—efficient and soulless.

Humans go out into the cosmos because they
need more space to think and breathe.

★ ★ ★ ★

There is more ice in the universe than all the planets put together.

★ ★ ★ ★

Knowing all of reality will be possible when the
barriers of time have been obliterated.

The individual future is tied to cosmic humanity.

★ ★ ★ ★

He who seeks infinity does not need his eyes to see.

★ ★ ★ ★

Either with imagination or with a special ship, navigate the cosmos with love.

Artificial intelligence can transport us to new dimensions or leave us in oblivion.

★ ★ ★ ★

We call *supreme* the infinite singularity that gave rise to the whole.

★ ★ ★ ★

Vicious arguments with infinity can be finite and funny.

Intelligence gave sapiens the triumph over other species, but imagination will open the future, giving dominion over space and immortality.

★ ★ ★ ★

Scientific discoveries illuminate the unknown outside of time.

★ ★ ★ ★

Being is the manifestation of intelligent life in the cosmos.

Never forget life is a system tending to perpetuate itself even if demands to eat you.

★ ★ ★ ★

What benefits the body benefits the brain but not always the mind.

★ ★ ★ ★

Who leaves as human returns as a Martian.

The person who returns from space
is never who went there.

★ ★ ★ ★

The day humans reach the bottom of the Universe, they will have touched the edge of their consciousness.

★ ★ ★ ★

An entire universe can germinate from a pebble.

A nebula contains gases, stardust, plasma, and our great ignorance.

★ ★ ★ ★

In the universe, what remains in us from earth is the sky.

★ ★ ★ ★

Just as humans have sons, daughters, and grandsons that aren't always like them, not all stars, planets, and satellites are like the bodies they come before.

The cosmos changes, and we with it.

★ ★ ★ ★

Time sinks in black holes and in eternity.

★ ★ ★ ★

Conscious truth permeates minds and hearts, thus reaching the end of the universe—our own being.

The cosmic being carries in the body of his consciousness
the quantum evolution of the existent.

★ ★ ★ ★

In space, destiny is in you.

★ ★ ★ ★

When consciousness is ready, new forms
of matter will be perceived.

Clad in starlite, humans and robots will pass through the stars uncontaminated.

★ ★ ★ ★

If the stars did not speak, men would live in darkness.

AKNOWLEDGEMENT

This book is the result of many years of being upset, frustrated, disgusted, or delighted by events, readings, discussions, dreams, meditations or arguments, poetry, music, mathematics, news, wars, political conflicts and family discussions that have suffered the translation-transformation of the original into a synthetic proverbial format. I am indebted to all the authors I have read over the decades. I am also indebted to all those friends or foes, national or international political figures, who tried to harm me or others, because in the end they could not avoid blessing me. They can't even understand or imagine, but I love them all.

I have to thank Julia Kolbert, Exhibitioner of Sidney Sussex College, Cambridge, for the final editing and her many wise comments and suggestions: and last, but not least, Bianca, my patient companion and wife.

Pietro di Vietri
Menaggio (Como), April, 2021.

NOTES AND BIBLIOGRAPHY

As these proverbs were written in diverse places of the world, the bibliography used was according to the books available in those places.

Aurelio, Marco. Meditaciones. Translation, Ramón Bach Pellicher, Madrid: Editorial Planeta De Agostini SA, Printed in Spain, 1997.

Confucio y su Doctrina. Beijing: Editorial Nueva Estrella, 1995.

Coogan, Michael D., ed. The New Oxford Annotated Bible, Third Edition, with Apocryphal / Deuterocanonical Books. New Revised Standard Version. Oxford University Press: New York, 2001.

Epitectus, Moral Discourses of Epitectus. Editado por W. H. D. Rouse. London: J. M. Dent & Sons Ltd. Y London: E. P. Dutton & Co. Inc., 1933.

Gibran, Kahlil. The Prophet. New York: Alfred A. Knopf, Inc., 1985.

Grieco, Pietro. Li fu, Un poeta campesino. Barcelona, 2017.

Khayyam Omar, Rubáiyát de Omar Kayyam. Spanish Version, by Felix E. Etchegoyen, according to the French translation of Franz Tourssaint, 5th Edition. Buenos Aires: Editorial Guillermo Kraft Limited, 4th Edition, 1952.

Séneca, El Libro de Oro. Barcelona: published with the Seven books of Wisdom, Edicomunicación SA, 1999.

The Little Book of Chinese Proverbs. Compiled by Jonathan Clemens, Edition published by Barnes & Noble Inc., by arraignments [A9] with Parragon, printed in China, 2002.

Printed in the United States
by Baker & Taylor Publisher Services